Of Drought and Fire

Two Natural Disasters in Australia

Frank Prem

Wild Arancini Press
2024

Publication Details

Title: Of Drought and Fire: Two Natural Disasters in Australia
ISBN: 978-1-923166-05-9 (pbk)
ISBN: 978-1-923166-31-8 (e-bk)

Published by Wild Arancini Press
Copyright © 2024 Frank Prem
All rights reserved:

No part of this publication may be reproduced, stored in a retrieval system, or transmitted in any form or by any means, electronic, mechanical, photocopying, recording or otherwise, without prior written permission from the publisher and author.
A catalogue record for this book is available from the National Library of Australia.

Cover Concept: Wild Arancini Press
Cover Image AI assistant: Adobe Firefly

Maps used in *Of Drought and Fire* were created by the Spatial Data Analysis Network (SPAN), Charles Sturt University, September 2024, using ESRI, (2024), ArcGIS Pro, 3.3.1, Redlands, CA: Environmental Systems Research Institute software.

Imagery data sources: Google Satellite & ESRI

Special thanks to Deanna Duffy of SPAN for her excellent map-making in the interests of poetry.

CONTENTS

Of Drought and Fire

Lagoon 5

A Koala In The Coalmine 105

After Words 243

    Index of Poems 245
    Author Information 249
    Other Published Works 250
    What Readers Say 251

Of Drought and Fire

Introduction

Of Drought and Fire is two poetry collections — *Lagoon* and *A Koala in the Coalmine*, written at different times (2006 and 2020) and about two different subjects — drought and fire.

It is also about diverse events that can be seen as the same thing, from two different perspectives — natural disaster and *un*-natural disaster.

The extremities of drought and fire are not rare events in Australia, but weather events and so-called *natural* disasters are increasing in both frequency and intensity. They are occurring around the globe also, now, with increasing frequency, in places unexpected and with impact unprecedented.

Year by year we are living in a diminished world. Year by year we actively diminish it further and wonder — when we look around us — *Why is it so What has happened to our world Oh dear. Oh dear.*

These collections of poetry represent a lived experience of severe drought and terrifying fire. The poems react and respond on a day-to-day and sometimes a minute-to-minute basis. It is possible they presage the world that awaits just around the corner.

Tomorrow.

VICTORIA

Lagoon

a song of the millennium drought (1997 – 2010)

Even a fish must breathe.

About *Lagoon*

Lagoon is a collection of poetry set around the halfway point in the Australian *Millennium Drought* which lasted from 1997 – 2010.The collection tells a twofold story.

The Broken River at Shepparton in Victoria (Australia) is prone to periodic flooding, with the area around its banks contoured over many years to form natural lagoons, or *billabongs*, functioning in their way as complete miniature eco-systems. Shepparton itself is a city at the heart of what is known as *canal country*, with mechanical irrigation feeding a substantial orchard industry and food bowl in the region.

By the year 2006, the effects of the massive, decade long drought had ravaged the lagoon lands bounding the river and *Lagoon* tells the story of the last days of one of these miniature eco-systems.

Told in parallel are stories of the *Millennium Drought* and its effect on people and the landscape. The new *normality* of water scarcity and irrigation restrictions imposed on whole communities across the land.

These are stories of heartbreak and hopelessness, with little prospect and no rain anywhere other than in the shimmering mirage of the horizon.

Yet, somehow, we survived, and these are those stories, told in free verse poetry, and written empathetically, to allow readers to share in and to touch these experiences for themselves.

For further reading about this and other Australian droughts, I recommend the Bureau of Meteorology's Drought Knowledge Centre. You can find it here:

http://www.bom.gov.au/climate/drought/knowledge-centre/previous-droughts.shtml

lagoon #01

the lagoon is growing
smaller

it is noticeable
now

springtime
has progressed
and there have been
no more
than a few meagre points
of rain
right through october

we walked a different way
today
when we let our dog
leelu
choose the path

we always go cross-country
and this time
we have cut
across the western face

I stopped us . . .

thought I saw a movement
that might have been
a fish

I hadn't thought there might be fish
in a lagoon off the *broken river*
but the ripples and the shadow
suggest life
in unsuspected places

dirty dreams and dry

and each new day
seems
a terrible wonder

a sudden
smite
and the well
is dry

a dirt-foul-brown stain
is a crack
through the heart

pray for water

to cleanse us

pray for water
for rain

pray

dreams like these
pain my eyes

lagoon #02

we bought a new camera
today

it's a pretty flashy unit
with more *snap*
than either of us
have ever owned before

and suddenly
the nature
of our walks with *leelu*
have changed

instead of charging off
down the path
loo-ie is now experiencing
stops and starts

a close up of some tree bark

point and shoot
at a tangle
of tall branches

pallid blanching
of dry grass
prematurely gone to seed

we only have one lens today
and the dazzling whiteness of a heron
that repeatedly parks itself
on the rising trunk
of a tree long fallen
is too distant
to satisfy

the bird never seems
to do more
than stand idly

patient
above the water

tomorrow
the second lens
will be deployed

all that is distant
will seem near

yellow mellow: desiccation north

on the radio —
in the car
when I was driving from work —
the weatherman was chatting
to Ms *Drive Time*

> *. . . and at home we say*
> *if it's yellow*
> *let it mellow*
> *if it's brown*
> *flush it on down . . .*

then
they went on
to talk about
using buckets at home

in the shower

especially for the water
that runs away
until the hot kicks in

just the way that *we* do

~

today the government declared
fifty percent —
maybe more —

of this massive continent
is subject to
special circumstances

there will be drought relief
for a further two years

each farmer will be able to buy
five thousand dollars worth
of counselling

will have
his borrowings subsidised
up to around a half
of a million

and maybe he will then
be able to decide
to leave the land . . .

his bowl of dust that used to
green up
in the spring

but there will be no
pressure
the decision will be up to him

and god
perhaps

or maybe —
this time —
it is the last of it

I heard that —
in the heart of drought —
four each week
find a brand new use
for a length
of bailing twine

on the edge of a ripe crop
of un-reason
and a harvest burden handed down
through generations

they swing

Of Drought And Fire

bitter kissed by a hot wind
from the north
that whispers desiccation

~

    some days

he said

    our family can go
    all day
    with just one flush

then gave
a forecast
for tomorrow

fine again

lagoon #03

I saw it entire
today

a fish leapt
out of the water

completely in the air

summersault
with pike

and then
shadows moving beneath
and ripples
circling above

no doubt about it
fish are in the lagoon
and moving around more

high visibility fish

and the heron
as well

perched on the same spot

I snapped some shots
but I'm not sure
if I've brought the creature
any closer

maybe it isn't meant
to be

amazing to see active fish
in such quiet water

a funny game

economics is a mystery sport

no need to wonder
about that

at a time when the only water
is tears

and the ground
under our feet
is broken

when the cattle fetch
nothing
and
a lamb
hasn't the price of its feed

when there are so many
heart-aching
broken
worried questions
aimed straight up
at the sky

with rust on the fences
and not enough hay to bail
in paddocks
that ought to be golden crop

a man
might do as well
to dance

feet
kicking dust in the air

let it fall

let it settle

coat him brown
and fill his ears and nose —
his mouth —
until he drowns
in the bastard stuff

it isn't *rain*
isn't *food*
isn't *enough*
and I say
economics
is a funny game
because
when I heard the news
about interest rates
I laughed
almost
until I cried

but in the end
even my eyes
stayed dry

lagoon #04

strange sight

the fish are easily visible now
I can see their shapes
below the water
but
they are surfacing all the time
as well

their great gulping mouths
are breaching the water
at regular intervals

I have a feeling
they might be drowning
in a perverse kind of way

because
I seem to recall reading
that the stillness of the water
and the fact that it is shrinking
at such a rate
means there is not enough oxygen
to support fish life

that's why
they break into the air

don't know if that's true —
it sounds dodgy —
but
there goes the fish
again

doing fruit

we spoke of doing fruit this year
it seemed the right thing to do
now we live in this
orchard valley
of flat lands and broken rivers

even the drought
shouldn't have stopped the year
because irrigation has always made
the peaches firm and round
the apricots run
sweet

the rivers look bare
showing bones

long dead trees and mud flats
seem somehow post-mortal
but there's still water coming through
and here at least
the year should have gone on
as usual

last night
we reverted to winter cool again

seems like each few weeks
there's another change
of season

a month ago
from out of the blue
the cool settled on the trees
white as snow
on a clear blue morning

there were two kinds of damage
they said
one will make the apricots fall
no later than a couple of days after

Of Drought And Fire

the other kind
might take a week
but the rest of the crop
will fall
shrivelled green and brown
and gone

I guess it's not our time
for doing fruit
there won't be much from around here
in the stores

won't be much
till next year
if the rivers are still running
by then

lagoon #05

this evening
there are two boys on bikes

they are right down low
at the water edge
riding back and forward
through the mud

having the time of their lives
and both filthy

back and forward
up to the axles

stuck

later
on the return part of our walk
they ride past us
on the path

look well pleased
with their efforts

the good news

good news good news

isn't it wonderful to get
good news
in the middle of calamity

they seem to blame *el niño*
for drying up the rain

and it's true
the boy child is no friend
to this parched land

it seems
sometimes
he loves us
too well
holds us close
in a warm embrace

we are his ecstasy

his love
might burn
but . . .

he is just an elemental
after all

a child

how can we blame him
for his zeal
or wish he loved us less
when we ourselves
have made him that way
our own inferno
but the weatherman said

it's good news

said

> relief will come
>
> this fire
> will only burn a short time
> not forever
>
> in a year
>
> or
> it may be
> two
>
> yes
> probably
> more like
> two
>
> the boy child –
> young niño –
> will turn away from us
> for awhile
>
> then we will be reprieved
> the rain
> will come
> must come
> to douse us
> close to drowning
>
> two years
> away
>
> only
> two more years
> away
>
> well
> no more than three
> at the most

lagoon #06

there is a duck
tonight
where the heron usually stands

I haven't seen this particular quacker
since early in the spring
when we caught a glimpse
of ducklings one day

but only the once

the rest is mystery

on the way back
a double take

where the duck was
is now the heron

no

no
it is not

it is a strange bird —
white body
black head

perhaps the duck
has transmogrified itself

I finally spot her
further up the tree snag

there has been a dislocation
in my absence

sacred ibis
appear to rule

for tonight
at least

factual oblivion

fact:

the government had a meeting today
to discuss the water crisis

~

fact:

the head of the rivers commission said

> *this drought is the worst*
> *in a thousand years*

~

fact:

the prime minister said

> *well*
> *no one can know that for sure*

~

fact:

the prime minister said

> *that wasn't meant literally*
>
> *it was just*
> *an expression*

~

Of Drought And Fire

fact:

the prime minister said

> *yes*
> *we know it's serious*
> *but it's not as bad as that*

~

fact:

the dams in the rivers system
are down
to eighteen per cent of capacity

some are less than that

~

fact:

one hundred massive ice bergs
are drifting north

leaving antarctica behind them

~

this may not be the worst
in a thousand years

who am I —
after all —
to doubt the prime minister

but there are some out there
not waiting
to find out for sure

they are diving in
decisively
not drifting
towards oblivion

like the rest of us

lagoon #07

there is no difficulty finding the fish
today
two are puddling in the shadows
on the near side of the lagoon

large fish
the line of them
is clearly displayed

great mouths gaping
when they periodically rise
to kiss the air

I don't know what kind they are
perhaps redfin or cod
more likely carp

but I am in no hurry
and will know
soon enough

the trenching left by boys
on their bikes
three weeks ago
is now metres
above the edge of the water

it won't be long
before the fish
are dry
and their identity established
beyond doubt

different rivers

we are on different rivers here

>I suppose you knew that

>yours
>is the broken
>while we
>are part of the goulburn and murray
>system

>there's a bigger flow for us
>and we still get ninety per cent
>of our allocation

>we've taken twenty-five head of cattle
>from down your way
>and put them in with our herd

>and while we can still irrigate
>it seems sensible to keep milking
>as many as we can

>did you see the new ute . . .

>marvellous vehicle

>utes are a funny beast now
>all of them come with a fat
>silver roll-bar in the back

>the old one was ok
>but
>this one doesn't cost much more
>to lease

>and anyway
>the missus is paying for it

yeah
did I mention
we're doing ok still —
compared to most —
but
it's her money putting bread
on the table

and she's the one paying
for the lease on the ute

it's funny to think
what a social worker might want
with a leased utility vehicle
but that's the way it is
and if it wasn't
then
ninety per cent water allocation
or no ninety per cent water allocation
I think we'd be going hungry

it's been a long time
since I could feed the family
just from the cows

the missus
has to have a job

come and I'll show you
the new diesel motor we put in
to run the irrigation sprays

lagoon #08

I seem to be fascinated
by these wretched fish

instead of proceeding
on the walk this morning
I stopped
to look for ripples
and swirls

they were there
sure enough

one seemed to be stirring mud
in the shallows for an inordinate time
without moving away
so I moved to the water line
to see
frightening the heron
with the racket
I made

the fish was gone
in moments
of course

and soon
the water was being noodled
along the edge of a fallen log
a short distance into the pondage

my curiosity
is without relevance
beyond being a nuisance
to the pond life here

seamless liquidity

is it just me
or is there real irony here . . .

we have severe drought

no water

two thirds of all water consumed
goes to farmers
who irrigate

some farmers can no longer
irrigate

now
the water authority
has created sixty jobs

farmers
who can't irrigate
will fill the water authority jobs

I like a system
that fits it's parts together
so seamlessly

lagoon #09

I have been away
for a week

I hear rumour
of inclement weather
while I was gone

I left during heat
but there has been snow
and storm
in the time since

my return is —
again —
into heat

the water seems
about the same
around the lagoon
not higher
not lower

there are three ducks
happily foraging in the shallows
but no sign of the fish
today
just dozens of circling ripples
from a myriad
of insects

the banks have changed
though

surrounding the dirty water
that is seemingly responsive —
like a tide —
to the tug of weather
the banks are bearing
irish green

whatever moisture has fallen
in the last week
has taken flight
through the rise of thin grasses
and weeds

today
they are a verdant collar —
like a celebration —
in the face of poor odds

what I heard today

they're turning the water off
in the irrigation district

two thousand farms
in all

anyone
who hasn't planted
had better not

anyone
who hasn't bought water
from somewhere else
had better not

the water company
is owned by farmers

they're making the call
to sacrifice their own

no more will flow until
a torrent-pour
of rain

maybe
no more will flow
at all

the farmer I heard explaining it
sounded bitter
although
as a member of the board
he knew
there is no other way

~

at work today
I read a cheery e-mail
from a *drought worker*

she is newly appointed
and wants to say *hello*

the last one I met
needed counselling
to stop herself from crying
at the dusty end
of every day

~

and one last thing today —
I swear
I nearly laughed —

the storage readings
for a list of dams
had fallen
by a margin

the same amount
for each separate storage

except for one

it was holding it's own

steady
under pressure

the capacity of others fell
but *lake eppalock*
stayed the same

I guess
it is hard to accurately measure
the amount or rate of water loss
from a two percent
holding level

lagoon #10

it is easy to fall into assumptions

I have been assuming
that my recent rumination
has been about
a drying lagoon

I should know better

what the dictionary tells me
about lagoons is

> *la goon [luh-goon]*
>
> *an area of shallow water*
> *separated from the sea*
> *by low sandy dunes*

or it could be

> *any small pondlike body of water*
> *esp. one connected*
> *with a larger body of water*

the possibility I like best
though
is this one

> *an artificial pool*
> *for storage and treatment*
> *of polluted or excessively hot*
> *sewage, industrial waste, etc*

yum

but my shrinking body of water
is none of these
and I should have known

it is a

> bil.la.bong [bil-uh-bawng —bong]

maybe
this version

> *a branch of a river*
> *flowing away from the main stream*
> *but leading to no other body of water*
> *a blind or dead-end channel*

I've seen these
but
mine is not this

an alternative is

> *a creek bed holding water*
> *only in the rainy season*
> *a dried-up watercourse*

not quite I don't think

it better be the last option

> *a stagnant backwater*
> *or slough*
> *formed by receding floodwater*

yes

that seems best

the area around the river
is surrounded by depressions

I can easily imagine them filled
by an overflowing river

harder to imagine
the river actually raising itself
to those lofty heights

so
my lagoon
is a slough

is a billabong

stagnating
as it dries

now I know

more like custard

the moon
when it rose the other night
was thick
in its colour

some nights
it looms pale

cream cheese

other times
more like cheddar

but this cycle
is thicker

deeper

with half the state
burning
this full moon of december
is smoked custard

lagoon #11

today
I think I identified the fish

his name is
fred . . .

no
only joking

I think it's a carp

I saw quite a lot of one specimen
up and out
of the water
and I know carp love to do that

I injured my knee
yesterday
and so my attempt
to subtly approach
the water
turned into a kind of
stiff-legged stagger
down the bank

rather noisy
in the end

it resulted in a mighty
whoosh
of water
as the fish powered away
towards the middle
of the billabong

there is still some green
around the edges of the water
from the last rain

perhaps it is holding its own
against the drought
but today
the temperatures are high
again

it seems an unequal contest

wrongness and sun

we stopped to look
early in our morning —
almost before
we'd properly opened our peepers —
to see the sun rise

liquid orange

molten heat

it is the smoke
of course

all too soon
we are burning
again

it seems moments
since the last fires
were put out
but
again we are stopped
by the sight
of the sun

to watch it shimmer
through the haze blanket
is to wonder
about the rightness
of things

lagoon #12 — zen fish

today
there is a breeze and —
I think —
it may be a tiny bit cooler

you and I sat
to watch
for the shape of fish
but
only saw vague ripples

you wondered if
they only surface
for me

know themselves
to be the subject
of my contemplations

perhaps

in the end we agreed

seeing the fish
isn't important

the act of contemplation
makes them as real
as if they were here
before us

watching weather (in time for christmas)

yesterday
at lunchtime
we were thanking the stars
for air conditioning

it was dry and hot
with bushfires ravaging
half of the known world

gloom and doom
and heat
everywhere we turned . . .

and then it rained

we smiled a lot

spoke lightly

you took photos of the sun
through cloud
and cooling breeze

I heard the neighbour laugh

her husband was watching
the activity of cloud formations
on the weather radar

following
the isometric movements
or whatever they're called

the meteorology
of a day
on which it rained

happy christmas

happy joy

it has rained

lagoon #13

a patina is still present
but the green
is a further distance
from the water now

the colour
has begun to seem
leeched

as though the *intensity*
of the hue
has retreated
back into the earth
while the soil
is still soft enough
to be receptive

ripple upon ripple
gentle moving
concentrically away
from each movement
of water-boatmen
or other such insect life
as inhabit pools
that are so
still

but not yet stagnant

life clings
in the expectation
of another outburst
of rain

hope risen (from a single fall of rain)

I try
but it is hard
to stop hope rising

yesterday's rain . . .

such a *joy*

and I want . . .

everyone wants
for it to go on

the papers are full
of the easing
that rain has brought

to fire
in *gippsland*
and *mansfield*
and the small town —
valhalla —
away up in the hills

the long-range weather man —
a strange
and almost mystical character —
has plumbed his wells
and divined
each future trace
of possible precipitation

he has emerged to declare —
free of charge —
for the wonder and benefit
of farmers

    it's only a month

he says

*just one more month
until it rains a rain
to drive this drought
away*

as I am spilling
the water
that pooled overhead
yesterday —
trapped in an awning —
I am hoping
with each drop
that splashes to ground

this could be a portent

and in a month

maybe less

it will rain like a flood
to wash us clean

I am hoping for joy
through water

and hope
has lightened my heart

lagoon #14

the sky has reached down —
grey laden —
to surround me
and the dog
leelu

the taste
is rancid ash

today the fires are burning
somewhere else

not close
but
the effect is a sensation
of nearness

a visceral impact

the water
in my personal lagoon
looks thin
and it is *still*

no fish splashing
no water-boatmen making ripples
no heron
or duck

even the breeze
has abandoned it

we are all oppressed
by the knowledge
of fire

back-burn lottery

there are still fires

we can taste them
in the morning air

a pungent undercurrent
to the first chortlings
of a magpie morning

a filter of restraint
cast over the laughter
of kookaburras

even snow —
that strange
white-ice substance —
at christmas
and a fall of liquid abundance
from the sky
could not put out all the flames

there is fire burning yet

the papers tell of a chance
to exploit the temporary cool

volunteers will burn
one hundred thousand hectares
to clear the scrub
between containment lines

in a few days
the heat will return
and the main fire
will meet
and extinguish
the back-burn
what a strange game
this is

Of Drought And Fire

a fight of fire
against fire

with a hope
for favourable wind

fair weather

and a better cast
of the die

lagoon #15

it is dislocating

I have not visited the pondage
for a time
that is weeks
rather than days

and I have had to take
to asking
what *you*
might have seen

but the lagoon
is *my* interest
not yours

and you can only tell me
that it is smaller

can only describe
disembodied ripples

it is my task
to imagine
the rest of the story

a departure by the boy child

there was talk again
today
of el niño coming to
a conclusion

like the end of a season
or an equinox

how will we know —
I wonder —
when it has occurred

will a *wet* begin

it is late
and I should be asleep
but I am up and thinking
about the boy child

the wind is sounding
and in the west —
the quarter from which
we get our weather —

they have had hail
and lightning

deluge rain

perhaps
he is leaving already . . .

perhaps

lagoon #16

such a difference
in just a short time

it is difficult to recognise the lagoon
now

the ground that was covered
by water
has receded

it is larger than a puddle
and has a little time left
but
it has been ravaged

around the edges
there is a darker shading
where the ground is moist

a little wider
the green of *in-between* pond grass
of some kind
is thriving on the borderline
between dry and wet

wider still
the colour has been leached
from the grass
that was itself at that in-between point
when water levels
were higher

the time when I
first looked down
on this water
two fallen trees
were mostly submerged
a heron and some ducks perched
at the base end of the trunks
above the water

now
I can study the entirety
of the trees

there is little concealed
below waterline

this sad phenomenon
is a fascination

rocket seeds and a helpful drip

you are picking seed-balls
out of lettuce
coloured in shades of orange
and brown

and we take a moment
to marvel
at nature

this is the first season
of our garden

it is only modest
but
every night
there is an offering
with dinner
and now the roquette
has gone to seed

we walked
this morning
to the river

brought back to home
a bucket filled with sand

suddenly
propagation is proceeding

seeds to seedlings
then to plants

I keep fiddling
with the water system

it is a small responsibility
but one that aches in me
as an urgent
obsessive pain

Of Drought And Fire

plastic fittings
somehow
don't seem to work right

this time it is a burred
and thread
hose-joiner

last time it was clearly
more
a problem of my thinking

but we are in a drought
you know
and the water needs to drip
exactly as required

we don't want to waste
any wandering drop
and otherwise
I don't suppose
I would do anything
at all

you look so
of-the-earth
in dirt
and dust
and smudges

and I
want to claim
at least
a modest contribution
to be a part
of the adventure

lagoon #17

it rained yesterday

a good rain
that lasted a couple of steady hours

and you can see the effect

you can smell it

the plants are clean
the trees
have released eucalyptus
into the air

dust has settled
and the air itself
is at ease
untroubled by excessive heat
and the accustomed oppression

even on the lagoon
there is a difference

two ducks have returned
one on a tree
the other swimming rapidly away
from my side of the water

they are reassuring
these ducks
but I wonder
what difference has yesterdays drink made

a centimetre

less

there is no run-off
from the rain
to boost the water level

Of Drought And Fire

all of it has been soaked up
by thirsty ground

gaping cracks in the clay
have not been closed

no
yesterday was a cleansing drink
but I wonder what is needed
to satisfy the hunger
for water

carol birds

there is a mudlark
in the branches of the tree
that overhangs our walking path

a mudlark
and two magpies

also
a mynah
of no particular status

~

magpies
are the first sound
of most mornings

their carolling
announces light
and sun

a presage to awareness
of the dry

often it will be a lone singer
mellifluous
through the gradual withdrawal
of sleep
and the imperious encroachment
of day

I watch them in the park
walking in groups
through parched grasslands

on the hotter days
panting
with beaks agape

yet
in the early light
at least one
will sing again

to call me
to the day

lagoon #18

you wondered
this morning
if the fish
might already be dead

there is little water left
no depth

and so
very still

perhaps it heard you
for there was movement
out in the centre

a large breaking ripple
of confirmation

so far
it is only
an uncomfortable drought

not yet
death

hope rage

they are feeble attempts
but
with each
constipated
droplet
that sounds on the roof
we feel lighter

more joyous

we tell each other
how clean everything looks

comment
on the freshness
of the air

and we marvel
at drop-patterns
in the dust

dust
after the best
this paltry storm
can conjure

I want to rage
about the futility
of these few drops

kick and stamp
and shout

roar
the despair I feel

the dismay that is all around
but

I cannot

for every inadequate
isolated
fool of a raindrop
brings me undone
in a surge of hopefulness

and I listen closely
for each strike of water
on the tin
above me

lagoon #19

it is hard to explain
the affinity

all around
are depressions in the ground
that have been —
in the past —
billabongs of the *broken river*

after each flood
water has occupied
the low-lying ground
creating sequences of small lakes
and ponds

all now empty

but for this one pool
that I pause to watch
and study

day after day
and sometimes
at intervals of weeks
I compare what I see *now*
with what *was*
at my last passing

the shrinkage
the fish
heron ducks and mudlarks

the insect boatmen
and random rising bubbles

I almost want to embrace
the whole shallow catastrophe
but instead
I measure the shrinkage
and wonder
when will floods return

what place will this be
when all the billabongs
are full
and the river
is less broken

ageing optimism

they have built
a nursing home
just down the street

it has gone up
in no time

and now
they are landscaping

funny how
even in the middle
of the worst dry
we've ever known
it is still ok
to plant grass
and to water it

in the middle of the day

perhaps
they have wiser heads
than mine

but these planners
of *old folks* homes

surely seem
optimistic

lagoon #20

today I've counted the trunks
of four different trees
that criss-cross the waterhole

I hadn't noticed all of them
before

last night it rained again

quite a heavy downpour
and I was glad to be awake
in the early hours to hear it fall

it is tempting to say
that a single fall
makes no difference
but that's not really true

for the ducks have come back

this morning
in the lee
of one of the fallen trees
there are three of the placid
brown ducks
on the water

wild and timid
they had a hatching
in spring
but then disappeared quickly
and these will likely vanish
again
within a day

but
for the moment
I can rejoice
in their re-appearance
each time it rains

two heats

it is the hottest day
of the year

the bare earth
seems ready to crumble

cracks widening
almost as we gaze at them

to be out in un-aided air
is to feel a dry
baking
heat

inside the house
cloying moisture clings
to brow

to arms

dampens underwear

broils

yes
on the hottest day
of the year
we have both kinds
of heat

and in the distance
thunder
snarls a disgusted rumble

so very
very
understandable

lagoon #21

weeks ago
I wrote about spooking a fish
in the shallows

it splashed and ducked away
rising some distance off
beside the trunk
of a fallen tree

it doesn't seem so long ago

I can stand beside the log now
stroke my hand
across the old wood

there is no splash left
where I am standing

a strange season

they are going to turn
the drinking water off
in benalla
at the very first
next drop
of rain

it sounds a foolishness

as soon as rain falls
they'll begin carting water
in tankers
for the rural city
of roses

it is because the drought
has brought supplies
down low

and because the fires
that are burning victoria
have filled the reservoir
with ash
fallen like snow
from the smoke clouds
that turned sunrise
to orange

sundown
to blood

and now
at the first positive sign
they will turn the water off
and start handing it out
in bottles

this summer
has grown into
the strangest
of seasons

lagoon #22

I couldn't believe the sight
today

it seems sudden
from one glimpse
to the next

there is hardly anything left
in the waterhole

there must be
I suppose
enough depth
in the centre for the fish
but
it is a confronting change

all through this little area
are ex-billabongs

depressions that
were once full of water

deeper than the height
of a man

locals say
it used to flood here
two or three times
each year

I can't imagine it

can't imagine
that it will ever flood
again

and my little hole
is not far
now
from gone

rain child

last night
the sky broke

rain fell

as it hasn't fallen
in recent memory

we had to rise from our beds
to make adjustments

the wind
whipping the awnings

rain
making them sag
under the weight
of water

the air was cool
almost cold
and when I shivered
it was a thrill

this morning
moist clouds replaced the sun

heavy
and grey

now
at mid-morning
the sky is bluest blue
crisp and clear
in its colour

it looks
optimistic

and I wonder
were they right
are we seeing the back
of the boy child

will he leave us for awhile
taking the baking heat
and cracking dryness
with him

is this rain a harbinger
of *la niña*

the time
of the girl

questions
questions

enough

today
is for a clarity of blue
not questions
about the precocious children
of weather

lagoon #23

sometimes
I find myself wondering
in absentia

what is happening
down there
at the water

did the last fall
of rain
make a difference

am I right
in my assumption
that it is only a delay
of the inevitable

not in *dreams*
but
in *imagery*
I see moving lines
of high-water dampness

increasingly skeletal
bones
of old wood

trees long ago fallen

I watch in my mind
the proud
or desperate
thump of a fish-tail
breaking the surface

I wonder
what will be
the reality
of the next encounter

no drought

there's never a drought
in psychiatry

our doors are always open

the beds always full

last week it was *seclusion*
for a woman

a big and burly farmer's wife
with an attitude

their farm is going to go under
because you can't feed dairy cattle
on bullshit
and empty grass

in tough times
farmers string themselves up
or take to eating the outpouring
of a shotgun
rather than betray their ancestors
or their children
by failing
on the land

and *this* woman . . .

well . . .

she has read all the stories
and had a crack
at doing the deed

at hanging herself

not quite serious enough
to make sure she wasn't found
but close

Of Drought And Fire

today
it is a different story

a young boy
from off a farm

went away to *warrnambool*

got in with a bad crowd
onto the drugs
and into debt

fifty thousand dollars worth
and nothing to show

all his cronies
sold what he bought
for next to nothing
as soon as he turned
away from them

and back home
he is milking
morning and night

sleeping in between

gotten irritable
but . . .

that *can't* be anything to do
with illicit drugs . . .

can it

he has had no
opportunity *yet*
to try to take
his own life

the parents think
it is about the debt

I know better
but
it's not *my* call to make

anyway
they've sold their
water rights

those
are worth a good penny
in this drought
and they will sub-divide the farm

the parents will end up
all-right
and they'll pay out the debts
for all four of the kids

that should see them through
and besides . . .

when you're *nearly sixty*
what else
are you going to do

it's a good job
they don't have to stay
on the land

a *very* good job

in psychiatry there is never
a drought

lagoon #24

it must have reached a point
called shallow

the dwindling pond —
almost a puddle —
has changed colour

it has gone from the greenish-brown
of a murky bottom
to rust red
right across the surface

we stood to watch
for a long time
but nothing seemed to move

just stray bubbles rising

something glugging
deep down
in the muck below

I keep expecting
to find fish
gasping

or dead

afloat on their sides
at the waters edge

but there's nothing

they seem to have
evaporated
along with the healthy colour
of mud

salvation (before the distribution of voting preferences)

suddenly

wetter than the thirteen inches
that they got up north
from the cyclone

more saturated
than the flatland around the yangtze
where the flood raged

louder
than the storm
that came late
but beat all-buggery
out of north america

we are saved

all our water woes
will be fixed
forthwith

ten billion dollars
was what I heard mentioned

climate change
has been discovered
and we're warming
towards solutions

    brother

    sister

    we
    will
    be saved

Of Drought And Fire

the government has found us
the planet
the hemisphere
the continental land mass

the north of us

the south

never mind the nay-sayers
never mind
yesterday

this is now

let hope rise

the election will be in november

don't forget
when you vote
you heard the good news here first

ok

lagoon #25

the spoonbills
are elegantly white

out of place
amid the mud and mirk
of the shrinking water-hole

the red-mud colour
has been dispersed
with the wind

perhaps it was
an algal bloom

I don't know
but I note the way
it has assembled itself
in a kind of ring
around the perimeter

waiting a chance
to breed into the centre again

a flight of fancy
while I watch the dazzling white birds
striding through the modest water
that rises not quite as high
as feathers

their bills are busy

backward and forward
backward and forward

it goes on
regardless of heat
and algae

despite the *dry*

it goes on

a bucket standard

the radio is taking talkback
about the drought

a physiotherapist has rung in

> *well*
> *the usual bucket*
> *holds about nine litres*
>
> *but people are going out*
> *and buying bigger buckets now*
>
> *the natural thing to do*
> *is to hug it to yourself*
> *when you carry it*
> *but they're too heavy*
> *and would-be water-savers*
> *are injuring their lower lumbar areas*
>
> *developing a condition*
> *we've started calling*
> *bucket-back . . .*

the garden looks wonderful

lush and green

you have created it
from nothing

this very year
in the middle
of the heat
and the dry
nine litres at a time
and love
and joy

a standard-size bucket
has been sufficient

lagoon #26

I can't help but smile

this morning there is a crowd
perhaps even
a gaggle

two herons
three spoonbills

an ibis

all beak-ing their way
around the waterhole
at pace

a veritable frenzy

they're able to walk
from end to end now

the water has dropped
far enough
to allow full concentration
on the job at hand

one spoonbill
is a standout

he has a black bill
and an unruly hairstyle

yellow feathers rise
in a shock
at the back of his neck

as though he is related
to a sulphur crested cockatoo
or at least
shares hairdressers
with such a gang
of reprobates

Of Drought And Fire

it is fascinating to watch
these large white wading birds
on a pondage I always thought
was better suited
to ducks
and swimmers

rain traces

the storms have arrived

in this geography
as the summer wanes
we get storms

each night
on the news
the weather tracker
shows where there has been lightning

where it has sparked fire

where there is prospect
of rain

we have had some rain

on more than one occasion
there has been a downpour
a lovely *tattoo* sound
to fall asleep to

in the mornings
after
eucalyptus aromas fill the air
as the trees release precious oils
like a celebration

but this is not a promise
it is only a play
brought by a fluke of timing
of the seasonal cycle

I will not believe
until the water rises
to lap at my feet

Of Drought And Fire

until the billabong
is more than a dry depression
so thirsty
it swallows random rain
without a trace

lagoon #27

it is a difficult image
to get out
of my head

I have avoided the writing
for days now
but . . .

it remains

such a *small* pondage now

I have seen —
from the depth of water
measured against a spoonbill leg —
that it is shallow
all the way across

mere inches

but the fish
are an extraordinary sight

pools ripple
in a dozen or more places
signs of the cold creatures
in constant motion

on the banks
in only half-coverage of water
the big ones lie
swishing their bodies —
sinuous
and without purpose —
from side to side

half their oversized bodies
above the water

they are muddling in muck
and it is as confronting a sight
as I
have ever seen

the farmer's march

and now it is almost past february

I am surrounded
by the flashing strobe
of lightning

the agitation of thunder

from here —
bedded in the heart
of the month —
they say
it will be *march*

yes
in *march*
we will see the end
of *el niño*

the bravest have announced
the very date
of his un-hastened retreat
after so many wasteland years
and from my trembling seat
I can almost believe them

yet
today I heard tell
of another deadline

farmers —
dairy
grain
beef —
have made their play

Of Drought And Fire

sown crops
and have done
whatever farmers —
desperate in their last hopes
and dire straits —
have always done

and it has been declared

> *in march*
> *the rain must come*

I hesitate in my celebrations
for
light shows and noise
can be performed dry

while march
is a race
run so very close

lagoon #28

it resembles a desolation
now

the nondescript weed
that has grown in the aftermath
of water
is a sickly shade of green
and stands as tall as a man

like a pestilence
surrounding the last of the pond
and together with the brown algae
suggests stagnation

the fish are evident
in clusters
gathered where the floor of the pond
dips slightly
to accommodate a bare centimetre
of more water

when I walk this way
to see what is left
I carry a sickly sensation
in my stomach
before the first glimpse

I am almost at the stage
of wishing I could not visit
any more

no need to witness
the *coup de grâce*
but
I am drawn to this

there is nothing to be done . . .

the pond will dry

and yet

this small verse
may be a larger sum
than nothing

normal wonder

ha

canberra has been buried
by ice

well
a massive hail storm anyway

about a metre deep
in places

filling shops and houses
meeting places
and centres of discourse

the biggest storm
in years

but here . . .

we had clouds
on the horizon

light-shows and grumbles
but not that good
wet stuff

I drove past a water-channel
two days ago

they were doing flood irrigation
around the fruit trees

the channel was full

water
was lying on the ground

and I felt

.
.
.

helpless

I have been feeling that way
a lot

I wonder if the rain
when it comes
(and
surely
it must come
one of these days)

but
when it comes
I wonder if it will
wash away
the helplessness

leave me
you
everyone
feeling on top of things

as though we have made
the right decisions

I wonder
will the rain
change everyone's life

anyone's life

back to
normal

I wonder what that
would feel like

lagoon #29

it has come more quickly
than I'd expected

less than a day
since my last visit
they are revealed
in a miserable totality

.
.
.

while we approach
along the walking path
a young boy —
a teenager —
is leaving the remnant billabong

mud
coating hands and legs
as he rides by
on a bicycle

he has been wading
and dabbling

a few fish —
un-loved carp —
are dead on the shoreline
but these
don't arrest the eye

it is the ones in the air
that make my breath catch

for they have been mounted —
mouth first —
onto branches of the fallen trees
that create the boundary
and structure
of the waterhole

they hang —
still and dead
but water-fat and shining —
only recently removed
for display

the boy calls a cheery
hello
as he rides away
smiling

.
.
.

I can see
one ripple

a sole escapee
waits to be claimed
by drought
or some
yet more unspeakable
misadventure

parched harvest

the hints
that it may be going
or perhaps
gone
keep getting reported

tonight though
I drove home from my work
a different way
and
maybe it is the time of year —
a seasonal thing —

or maybe
they were old . . .

I don't know
but
I passed a small mountain
of uprooted trees

taller than I
have ever seen

uprooted
and heaped together
like a massive bonfire stack
before cracker-night
on the fifth of november

and across the road
pears hung
yellow and over-ripe

beautiful

doomed

the trees un-watered

Of Drought And Fire

their leaves parched
and curled

this is orchard country
peopled by folk
who love their trees
as they do their children

and I cannot believe . . .

no
I cannot quite believe
the worst
is over

lagoon #30

desiccation has occurred
overnight

the plump
water-fat fish bodies
have sagged and shrivelled

and the waterhole
this strangely fascinating study
of heat and time
and detached involvement
has shrunk with them
since yesterday

it is no more
now
than a muddy bog

a death hallow
with disturbing shapes
suspended in ghost branches
and a handful of pathetic corpses
abandoned and half buried
in the wake
of a no longer existent
waterline

the lone ibis
stalking the remnants
of this distressed summer
can have no further reason
to return

seasonal content

the season has changed
without doubt now

in the space of a week
it has passed from *doona-summer*
to winter cold
and back again
as the nights have cooled
inconsistently

from shorts and no shirt
to *tracki-daks*
jumper
socks and slippers

each evening
has been starry
and cool

the night before last
it rained
a brief burst
but substantial

today
the rain
has not stopped

the season has changed
for sure
and the predictions
have also come true
el niño has departed
for parts unknown

whether it is
for a long time
or short

whether la niña
is to replace him

whether the drought
is now passing

no-one can know
but
the water I feel
on the collar of my jacket . . .

the puddle that I can splash
with my boots . . .

are confirmation
of a brand new season
and . . .

right *now*

I feel content

lagoon #31

we are a solemn gathering
today

I stand at the top of the path
with you
looking down into the bowl

to me it is a forlorn sight
with the floor cracked open
like a crazed sore

scabbing
but too tender to touch

the fallen trees are a disquiet
in the thin embrace of silence

tall weeds —
still green on moisture
stolen from the drying corpse —
are a mourning crowd
leaning in
towards the heart of the bowl

one fish . . .

two fish
remain obscenely mounted

flags waving farewell
from grey branches

the rest
merging by degrees
into the exhausted soil
and the dust
of a memory

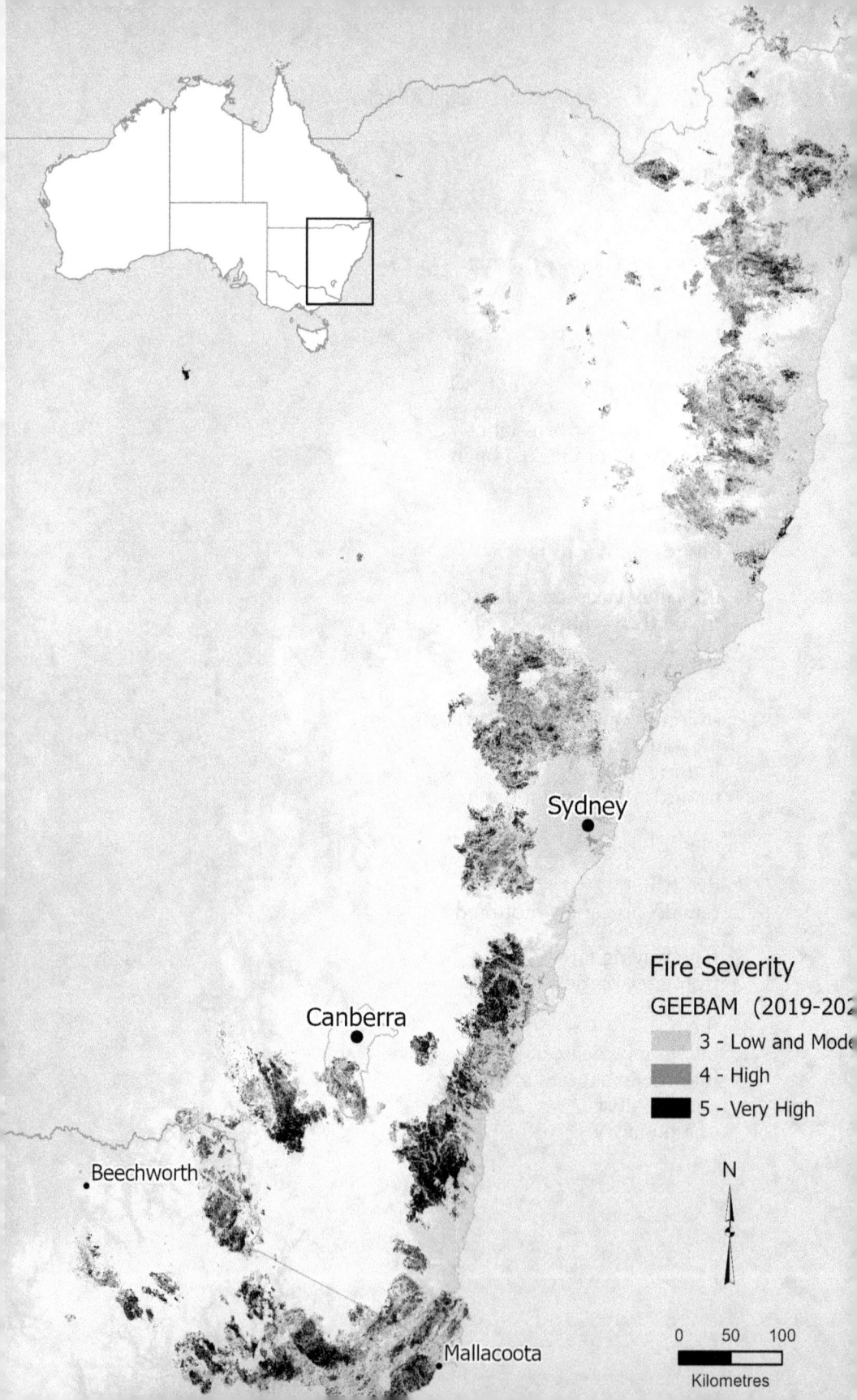

A Koala In The Coalmine

Australia Burning (2019 - 2020)

The thought I had was just a refugee.

About A Koala in The Coalmine

In late 2019 Australia began to burn.

First in New South Wales and in Queensland. We, in the south-east of the country, read stories and heard reports of our special places – Rainforests and National Parks – and vast tracts of the eastern seaboard in flames.

Houses and towns were evacuated, with some burned to the ground. Death and loss, yet again.

As a poet and author, I believed I had done my share of writing this kind of catastrophe when I penned the poetry of *Devil In The Wind* about the disaster of our 2009 Black Saturday fires here in Victoria. But, on New Year's Eve in 2019, I began writing the poem *a streaky river (for my face)*, and I found that I could not stop.

This collection, *A Koala In The Coalmine*, is the result of my own engagement with the calamitous fire disaster that beset the country in a wave of destruction that no Australian could have conceived were it not unfolding before our very eyes, every day.

The year 2020 later became synonymous with the outbreak of the COVID 19 global pandemic, but it began with the burning of my country to the point where the smoke obstructed the view from space, and Australian residents of this wonderful land had to take to small boats and flee, lest they be caught up in the conflagration and burned.

Refugees in our own land. An outcome not without its own bitter irony.

a streaky river (for my face)

every tear
is wept
in black

and tears . . .

there are
so many

cried dry

for there is an absence
here
of such water

day
is night
and the night
that is day
runs red
in anger

stand
and watch

that is all
that we can bring
ourselves
to do

for the sky
is raining fire
and the earth
beneath our feet
has sacrificed
all that it had
in vapour

green . . .

there is no green

no more

only this dust
that was
a forest

was it
yesterday

was it just
yesterday

I suppose
there must be rain
somewhere . . .

perhaps

and perhaps it falls
in plenty

I could pray
and
I *would* pray
for a wind
to blow it closer

but the only wind
like the only prayer
is just a fan
being waved
to build more fire

I shed
another streaky tear

a dry river

and I let it mark
my face

and we become (the thing that we denied) a refugee

the thought I had
was a refugee

I've had these thoughts
before

once in a boat
upon the waters
of an ocean

sometimes
as an idea
in the sky

but lately
I've been watching flame
licking at the leaves
on the trees

bringing darkness
when the sun
should shine

and I see photographs
in my newspapers

pictures
on the TV screen

of mamas
holding it together
the best way
that they can

of papas
crying

like the world's gone
mad

I count
the creatures
that aren't where
they should be
and my thought
is just a prisoner
to the knowledge
that the world has changed

there is no koala
here

no blue-tongue lizard

no wombat and
no kangaroo

I cannot see
a magpie

the kookaburra
is not laughing

no brown snake
or tiger

where is
the fairy wren

the wood ducks I remember
as a score

are there any left
I wonder

is there anywhere
that they might go . . .

in my mind
I can see
a desert now
where rainforest
always swayed

Of Drought And Fire

I see
a land
that was once
my home

and my thought
becomes
a refugee

who am I
who are we
when the things that make us
we
are gone

who am I
who are we
when the air
we took so much
for granted
is brown
and
is the night time
of our lives

what am I
what are we

I don't know
I don't know

I don't know

mellish street (tomorrow)

I look out
toward the space
where I know
the paddocks lie

mellish street
is safe
tonight

nothing going on
but a car
with one headlight

too noisy

yet the night
is calm
and there is no glow
on the hills
or the ridges

but neither is there peace
nor rest
even though nothing else
is stirring
and
there was nothing
to be seen
today

I can find no
tell-tale smell
in the air
tonight

but I know —
like the next beat
of my heart —
that it is coming

Of Drought And Fire

last time
it was on library road

the time before
mount pilot
was the blaze

on another occasion
we simply had to leave
because
the only air
that we could breathe
was a flame

was a fire

and it might be
as soon
again
as tomorrow

or
we may have to wait
till next week

but in the meantime
every picture
beamed into my head
is of sheets of iron
twisting

and the underworld emerged
to leap from tree to tree
and mile
after mile
either concentrating hard
and fierce

or just
too damned
gleeful

I am surrounded
by feelings
that make me bow
my head

like a death in the family

the death —
this time —
of all the things that I . . .

that *we* . . .

all the things
waiting for their burning
whenever the fire decides

I don't believe
there is a god
of weather
anymore

I can't believe
there is a god
of rain

but there should be
because I know
some people
are spending all
their spare moments
just praying

and as the world
tastes its own ash
as it gasps
I can't help feeling
that I am no better

for I say
a little thanks
that mellish street is all right
tonight
and we will open eyes
to the same
tomorrow

but
maybe
tomorrow . . .

maybe
for mellish street
it will be
tomorrow

blue and black and the bridge (on fire)

they are lighting
fireworks
in sydney

tonight
the old year ends

the next one
is just around
the corner

so many things
are just
around the corner

sydney
could not see
its own hand
in front of the bridge
only the other day

perhaps
a kind breeze
has blown the smoke
away
but
in any case
this
is australia

we have to put on
a display

have to
put on
a show
and I guess
that we have exceeded
like never before

Of Drought And Fire

I guess
we've made a success
from our own
hardship

I recall
in the nineteen sixties
(so old am I)
the astronauts
took photographs
of earth

green and blue
and white

an awesome image

a celestial queen

and I had never seen
anything
so beautiful

today
the pictures from space
are a blackness
that is framed
in red

and yellow

I don't suppose
they can show each flame
but
I know those flames
are there

and it is beautiful
in a way

a desperate
and sad
and weeping
kind of way

we are
a christmas decoration

a bauble
set to flame

and sydney
might find itself
in the firework lights

when the rockets fly
up
and up

and then
explode

a celebration
of fire
performed
with fire

I think I should step
outside . . .

watch the stars

maybe
a space station
and
an astronaut will pass

they all
still look beautiful
to me

and my memories
of blue and green
and white
of
a celestial queen

are still
for me
more precious than
glitter and explosions

setting the bridge
on fire

dreaming

I was not
asleep

I was
just
dreaming

all night long
about the hills
on fire

I was wondering
where
does meaning lie
when
we are burning

I listen to
the call for trees

new and many

maybe we should
plant them
now
to stop the changes
in our atmosphere

but
a handful
of leaves
doesn't seem
enough of much
to stop the demons
in their dancing

I was not asleep
do you
understand

Of Drought And Fire

but in my mind
my own feet
were alight

and I was wearing
the skin
of an old man roo

my heart beating
as one
with the fleeing

you cannot see
in the centre
of a fire

you cannot see
looking in
from the outskirts

you cannot see
through the black
and the brown
and the flames
climbing
high enough
to know
that yours
is the next one
coming

I leap
and I bound
in the black

is it night

I leap
and I bound
there is no
difference

I turn and I twist and
I turn around again

and still
it can see me
coming

until I stop

    (heart pound)

let the night
happen as it will

stop

    (heart pound)

give myself up
to the flame

and stop

    (heart pounding heart pounding
    heart pounding)

to wonder
if I
am alive
or am I still
just dreaming

from somewhere
beyond

but I think
that I wish

and I know
that I wish

that perhaps

this is only me
dreaming

deserving (better)

last night
I left the windows up

screen-doors
instead
of the glass

this morning
I have a house
that is filled with the taste
of burnt forest

the cockatoos
are squawking
in a kind of
croak-time cadence

rising
in pitch
to a screech

and the way
I hear

it sounds like a calling out
aloud
for mercy

but
the sun is up
again
today

it will be
fierce

it will be
relentless

so I'll leave
a little drink
in a bowl
beneath the plum tree

in case
they're thirsty

sad songs
play in my mind
as I look out
through
a middling blue
haze

some mornings
I have watched smoke
lazing
in little valleys
and some days
the hills around me
are distorted
by the thickness
in the air

I am reminded of
when I was a child
with chronic asthma
trying to know
how
to breathe
when my lungs
would not work

and I can feel it
again

the choking
the wheeze
the desperation for a gulp
of easy air

Of Drought And Fire

I hear the cockatoos
again
and I know
what they are asking

some days
I wonder

>   *what is it*
>   *that I have done*

some days
I know

I know
the answer

>   *nothing*

I have done
nothing

for too long

and too much

too
determinedly

I have done
nothing
to deserve anything
better

something (really)

new friends
are writing pen-letters

on a screen

I've never met them
before

but they are telling
their stories
of a world gone mad
and
I am reading

so
immediately
I am with them

immediately
I am there

and I can understand
what they tell me
of their grief
about the houses
and the land
and the forest
and
the animals

I can understand
when they describe
the blackness
in the middle of a day

and the wondering

what is going
to happen

it is just as though
I am standing
beside them

and still
I don't know
what I should say

but
they are friends
of mine
now

new friends
forged in a fire

and at least
they know
that I know

and that
is something
I suppose

in a world
suddenly
filled with uncertainty

knowing that somebody
out there
can hear you

well

that's something

yes
really something

a (prime) ministerial (possible) message

it might read
something
like this

>don't be alarmed
>
>don't be
>concerned
>
>this has happened
>before
>
>you know
>we are great
>survivors
>
>I am praying
>for you
>my dear
>brave people
>
>there is no one
>now
>never has there been anyone
>like you
>
>as I watched
>last night
>the fireworks
>across sydney harbour
>
>I found a moment
>alone
>just to contemplate
>
>and I concluded
>again
>we are a wonderful
>people

Of Drought And Fire

*we volunteered
once
for war
and this is just
such a fight*

*and
we want to be there
in the teeth
of the battle*

*and we
want to be there
beating back
at the flames*

*we don't give in
without a fight
and
I am right
behind us*

*I know
we will win*

*I know
you will fight*

*I know we will all
be proud
at the end
of the day*

*we
are sorry*

*all of us
are
sorry*

*for the losses
of life and of towns
and of property*

the bush

but at the end of the day
I will be
a proud man
to be the leader
of you
at such a time

so fight again
and fight strong

fight again
as long
as it takes

we are all
australian
and we have fought
before

you
are today's heroes
and you should know
that as I watched
the glittering lights
last night
across the harbour

I was thinking of you

of us

and I felt proud

we can all
feel very proud

looking away (from a trip I took)

I remember driving
over hotham's top

I think
it was a year
ago

the most terrifying drive
when looking
down the slope
at the side of the road
it seemed endless

the mountain air
was a beautiful thing
distilled
right out of
eucalypt trees

and on the other side
going downhill
from omeo
to metung

and
to bairnsdale

by then
we were in gippsland
and the forest
gave
slow way
to the sea

I recall
how green it was

and I remember
the chuckle
of a gold-bottomed creek

thinking
how nice it might be
to perhaps
live there

we walked on a beach

listened
to the washing
of the waves

I took pictures
of old driftwood
that held images
that looked a lot
like faces

.
.
.

now

I get to trace
the line
of that journey
on a map
with the tip
of my finger

orbost
and cann river

buchan
with its caves

mallacoota

the long stretch
of downhill highway
that took us
coasting
right to orbost's front door

but
I don't suppose
I will go there
again

I don't suppose
there will be much
left

and the images
staring back at me
from dead timber
will not seem
the same

in any case
I don't think
I
can face them

I don't really think
I *want*
to face them

think
I will have to look
away

pray for (a bottle of) rain

what will we do
without
water

we cannot
drink
brown dust

> we will sell the rights
>
> dig holes
> down
> into the earth
>
> draw it up
> into the tank
> of a truck
>
> send it to the city
>
> put it
> in a bottle
>
> sell it
> for the good
> of someone's health
>
> from fresh mountain springs
>
> you know
> it must be good
> for
> someone's health

what will we
do
for water

nothing
is falling from the sky

we're restricted
to using one hundred litres
a day

I can hardly wash my face
with that

what will we do
with no rain

> *we'll sell the rights*
> *to a water-mining*
> *venture*
>
> *make a dollar*
> *for the people*
> *of this state*
>
> *this*
> *is*
> *for*
> *the good*
> *of all of you*
>
> *we might ship some*
> *in a tanker*
> *across the ocean*
> *to china*
>
> *it's all being done*
> *with you*
>
> *at the forefront*
> *of our minds*

what will we do for
water
now
you know
there is not enough
to grow the grain

and today I see
that the country
has been set
on fire

what will we do
for its dousing

can you tell me

what can we do
to quell the flames

> *I'm sorry*
> *but a contract*
> *is a contract*
>
> *I'm sorry*
> *what do you expect*
> *me*
> *to do*
>
> *sorry*
> *I'm sorry*
> *but*
> *there's no good*
> *in you complaining*
>
> *you know*
> *you'll have to pray*
> *for rain*
>
> *in the end*
> *and always*
> *you will have to pray*
> *for rain*

we will bicker (until tomorrow comes)

the night . . .

last night
was filled with smoke

I know

I am coughing it up
this morning

and my backyard carries blue
above the green
and the gold
of dying grass

I find
I am still thinking of . . .

conducting

a conversation
that I had yesterday

more like
an argument
perhaps

> *where are they*
> *now*

he said

> *where are*
> *all those greenies*
> *who think*
> *we ought to leave*
> *the trees and bush*

*and don't want us to have
the cool burns
for forest management
in the autumn*

*they're not sticking their heads up
now*

when we're burning

a decision point

to enter into the discussion
with all my passion
and my feelings
and what I consider
to be my knowledge

should I throw it —
inflammable as it is —
on this ill-informed
ungracious
condescending
finger-point blaming
tinder

an explosion
of indignation at
lies and half-truths
and denialism

peddled
in the disgusting press
and swallowed whole like manna
to sustain the righteous

no

it is hardly worth the effort
to explain
again to clarify

to remind

and to remember
that all of us
would like
to wake up
in a familiar world
tomorrow

no
I let it go

and today
seems like it must be
a different
tomorrow
from what we hoped for
and wanted

all of us

today
is blue
hovering
as a tinge
above the green and gold

a tomorrow
for all of us
is here

and I wonder
how long
will we bicker

not here (when we burn)

they are waiting
now
on the beaches

four thousand
are stuck
in a holiday town

joe
is informal spokesman
for the township

says

> well
>
> we all crammed in
> to a recreation hall
>
> just before
> new year's eve
> when
> everything was first flattened
>
> people ended up
> sleeping
> in their
> cars
>
> and going hungry
>
> because
> we were running out
> of food
> and petrol
> and power
> and places for people
> and communications
>
> so we didn't know
> what was going on

or what to do

huh
you ought to try to tell
something . . .

anything

to a crowd of hundreds of people
crammed in
to a couple of rooms

and all of them moaning
while somebody's trying to tell them
what they need to know
without a P.A. system

.
.
.

I couldn't hear a thing
above
all the complaints

today
they are waiting
on the beach

three thousand of them
are tourists
stranded

one thousand
are locals . . .

stranded

there is a navy ship
anchored
a kilometre off the shore
ready to help out
with evacuations

but joe says

*we don't know
who
they'll be taking*

*we don't know how many
they'll let
get on board*

*and we don't know
how long
it will take*

*or how much time
do we have*

*we hear
that the weather
will turn bad
again
by tomorrow*

*none of us know
if we'll survive*

*and all they can say
is that
they need to work it out*

*and I suppose
that's true*

*yes
I know
that is true*

but the weather is not . .

you know

*the weather
is not . . .*

Of Drought And Fire

oh
the weather's just a bastard
like it's never been
before

and I don't give a damn
about the reasons
or the cause

the weather
is not on our side

not anymore

and I don't want
to be here
when we burn

nobody
wants to be here

when we burn

please

if we all
shed
one small tear
for
every little animal

that
would be beyond
half a billion tears
(so far)

and if we all had
another small weep
for the demise
of all the eucalypts

the world would have
another ocean
I believe

cry
another ocean
if you
please

bitter

wake up
to grey smoke
outside my window

the only colour
red
is in the pictures
of fire
that haunt my telephone screen

the birds
are all singing
so
I guess
they haven't heard
the official news

we are a catastrophe
now
a declared
disaster

and all the messages
coming in
advise
that we should run

but I'm not sure
that anywhere
is better
than anywhere else

the smoke is thick
and it tastes
of bitter fruit

heartbeat (leadership)

I have been reflecting
on leadership

what is the making
of a leader
in a time
of crisis

so many things
in recent times
have needed
leadership
~

there were boats
of refugees that needed
stopping

there was a man
who claimed credit
for that

he made the calls
and gave the orders

those boats
were stopped
~

there was a problem
with the budget
of the nation

too much
was being spent

    on welfare

*the old the sick
the unemployed and feeble*

*on building things
for posterity*

one man stood up . . .

no
it was many men
(some women too)
stood up
as one

willing to lead
in the cause

no decisions
required

not really

not when the need
for fiscal restraint
is (always)
so
self evident

and all those men
those many men
led
even if
there might be personal cost
to other folk
sometimes

such outcomes
are sad
but necessary

courage is required
from all of us

for this
is a matter
of highest faith
and budget surplus
must be achieved

~

there was a matter
of threat
to the foundations
of our nation

old ways
considered
not good enough
anymore

there was a man
who stood up
in the parliament

waved
a piece
of coal
to demonstrate

there could be
no change
to the old ways

his leadership
would ensure
that it stayed
so

~

such decisions
such
judgement calls

none of them
was small

but at heart
these were matters
of belief

decisions
made safely

at a distance

safe but
hard and fair
(depending
on perspective) . . .

~

fire comes
the nation burns

this is a challenge
to belief

there is no article left
of faith
that will not be burned
if it stands still

where
is the leader
we are needing

where is
the one we crave

I wonder who
will stand up
to show us all
the way

I wonder
who
will be brave

will *faith*
sustain them
or
will they be listeners
to the sound
of their own
hearts

a leader listening
to the sound
of all
our
hearts

the battle (do or . . .)

today is the day
(for the moment
at least)
that they say
might bring the creature
to our doorsteps

it will start out cool
then boil up
later on
into searing

looking out the window
the smoky haze
is not too bad
so far

though I can still taste
yesterday's plastic
in the air
and the stench
of burning rubber

mostly
what I notice —
making the ground
seem like
a carpet that has come alive —

are the flits
and the flights
of a cloud of small
blue butterflies

and we will stay

it has been decided

that
is our fire-plan

stay within
the township boundaries
though

we will not seek
to defend
at our door

there are places
to run if we need to
to be as safe
as anywhere else is

and we will do our best
to survive
along
with all our neighbours

I will go
to my workplace
in the afternoon
to undertake my regular shift

there are others
whose need
falls within my realm
of duty

so
let us all hold hands
for a moment

even across
the width
of the seas

beyond these burning skies

let us all hold hands
to feel
that we are
in this moment
as one
and together

and to pass
a little love

pass a little thought

pass a little strength
then
turn around

face
whatever comes
with all we have
and
do or die
my dears

do or die

what may come (we shall see)

all is quiet
on the news front

the fire map hasn't moved
(much)
in a day

the tweet-ing world
is alight
in it's own
peculiar way

voices voices
shouting
to be heard
on the subject
of australia

and of burning

the little blue
butterflies
don't care

the bees are still
tending flowers
on every weed
that's showing up
uncut
in the heart of the lawn

this
is a time
for not sweating
the small stuff

suddenly

almost *everything*
is
small stuff

ah well . . .

the navy is taking
refugees
off the beaches

the army
is refuelling
wherever it can

the air force
is dive bombing
with retardants

the war is on
god knows what
the big plan is

but
I do not

I make smaller ones

> *survive today*
>
> *do the best
> you can*

is my mantra

and the strangest thing
is needing to wait
for something —
some event —
to actually survive

because
the day is quiet

the air
is still

yesterday
when nothing actually happened
was
much worse

these are strange times

come-what-may
times

I look around
at my house and home
and
I like it

I will live
though —
if I must —
without it

come what may

we
shall see

hungry

the day
has become
a furnace

dry heat
buffets
against my face
and into my body

it is being pushed
hard
by a drying wind
that ruffles me
in the over-friendly way
that feels
like a police frisking

no part of me spared
and something
is taken away
with every touch

so
on a day like this
I keep a bottle
close
and I drink it
down
and
I drink it down

for this wind
is
forever hungry

I recall
a time
when I stood inside
on the floor
of a sauna room

the moment
just before water
was poured

the dry
of the air in my throat
back then
made it hard
to swallow

and today
too

I find this
almost
too hard
to swallow

no one (she said)

and at work
she comes
to ask me

>*is there any*
>*bush fire burning*
>*in my home town*

it is a little village
that she is talking about
and she lived there
for a while
as a child

a long time ago

before moving
here and there

before moving in
to the mental institution

and she still calls the village
home

calls it
the place
where her family lives

they have been dead
for many years
but
that doesn't matter

and is not real
on the days when her mind
transports her

I point
to a name

a very small
name
on the fire map

it sits
just on the right-hand side
of a thick black burn line

    oh

she says

    that's lovely

and then she asks

    is there anyone dead

so I tell her
there are nine
dead

twenty-one
are missing

    no

is her reply

    no-one is dead

    no-one
    is going to die

    they are all
    going
    to hospital

    no-one
    is going to die

sated

. . . and now
it is
a balm

the change
has come

and the breeze
holds the promise
of warmth
without burning

of comfort
gentled
upon my face

the change has come

for today
the danger
is gone

I raise my face
into the sated breeze

up
to the sky

close my eyes
and sigh

close
my eyes

relieved

the 101 ways (#79)

it steals
through the night
removing stars
from the sky

one
after
another

I wake up
and look around

immediately
the feeling

>*a building-up*
>*of irritation*
>
>*the sense*
>*that there is something*
>
>*that I need*
>*to sneeze*

I turn on the light
and . . .

for a moment
I believe
I am looking
through a veil
within my bedroom

another moment
until I know
that it is real

my breath
is shallow

Of Drought And Fire

from somewhere
a fog . . .

a pall

has come

settled
like a thick
stinking blanket
that has the taste
in it
of many deaths

all over the town
it has triggered
smoke alarms

a thick yellow
stench
within the lamplight
of street corners

poison gas
wafting about
on near-absent breezes

drifting
from nearby battlefields

I think
through an aching head
of the 101 ways
to die
by fire

a smoke shroud (of change)

how different

how
the same

a week
can be a lifetime

can be
a death time

can be a time
of change

.
.
.

of so
much
change

claustrophobic smog (cry the cockatoo)

the yellow tinge
of claustrophobic smog
continues to surround the houses
on my street

I
am trapped inside
hiding
from deadly vapours

and the light —
so strange —
is a late afternoon
in mid-morning

the light
is a jaundice
on the pall
that is this day

which is itself
a nightmare
we all
are dreaming

trapped deep
in a sleep
in a dungeon
of smog

even the cockatoos
the raucous
cockatoos
are weeping

the fog price

it is an eerie light
that shines
through filter smog

it has the colour
and stillness
of yellow

nothing more
for there is no
breeze

a delusion suggests
that
it is fog

mist

but no no
no
no

it is dry
to the throat

troubling
to the nose

too thick
to the taste
and on my tongue

it is
altogether
too
heavy

and I can't help
thinking

that this deathly stillness
is the future
we now hold
much dearer

normal (now)

I wonder

what is the current definition
of normal

there is
a little rain
today

it is a day
off work

the fire is not close

while the politicians
haven't found their way
yet
to fill my pages

but
the smog persists

neighbours
are scared
even without the galvanising
imminence
of evacuation

normal

well

I'm not sure

it was cool enough
last night
to pull a light blanket
up

but temperatures
will be rising again
by friday

people ask me

>*how*
>*are we going*
>*to live*
>*like this*
>
>*with our minds*
>*on edge*
>*hearts beating*
>*too hard*
>
>*looking up*
>*to not seeing any sky*
>
>*and feeling*
>*so helpless*
>
>*so*
>*afraid*

worry yes (but just a little pleasure)

I confess
I had a drink
tonight

I confess
that I had
two

you see
I've been cutting back
for the very good
of my health

and I've been
setting myself
up
for a personal
long future

but even today
when the fires
are quiet

if I step
outside
the door

the fog of smoke
curls heavy
around
my shoulder

and I wonder
what
is the justification
for self-discipline

what reason
have I
for restraint

a quiet day
a quiet
night
but tomorrow
the blaze
might take over

and care . . .

no
it will not care
if I am
sober

so
tonight
I've had
a little drink
of red

tonight
I had another
oh
yes
yes

tonight
I have drunk
as though
tomorrow
may not come

tonight
I have drunk
for *now*

I would hate
to go
without the taste
of what we
are fighting for

Of Drought And Fire

I would hate to go
with all the worry
and none
of the pleasure

all taken (by the day)

I don't have
asthma

no

I know what that is like
and
I don't have it

it's just
very
hard
to breathe

as though the air
is heavy
on my tongue
and in my throat
and
drifting down
toward my lungs

as though
I have been
working

much harder
than I actually have

and the exertion
has taken a toll

so
I puff a bit

and
I blow a bit

Of Drought And Fire

winded
as a draught horse
hauling a loaded
dray

I am lacking
stamina

lacking
some other
essential

or perhaps
it has all been taken
by the day

everything I have
taken
by these days

the blessing of (two mls) of rain

two and a half
millimetres
of rain

not much

maybe

but it's the first
we've had
since the second
of december

and it helped
to keep things quiet
for a day

the fires began
in september

there were
fifty three mls
for that month

in october
twenty-four

november
forty-three

december thirty-one
and a half

just one and a half
old inches
every month

not enough
to keep a wild rabbit
alive

but that little drop
that fell on us
yesterday
did the job

made it cool

slowed things
down

and while
I would love to get
a bigger drop

and I would love
to have it rain
for two solid weeks

while I'm waiting
for that to happen
I will settle
for this

a couple more
millimetres

please

to be (before the flame)

today
I believe
is an elemental day

there is stillness
in the air
but
I can feel a breeze

such
a gentle breeze
touching me softly
as it passes

so gentle . . .

how could it kiss
embers
into fire

and yet . . .

I look at the map
with its lines of arrows
pointing
here
and pointing there
to suggest the way
the wind blows

it changes
in the sketching
every hour

and so
every hour
the entrails
that predict our fate
must be read again

Of Drought And Fire

what altar
should I build
to the elemental
gods

what place of worship
for the wind
and the rain

and the heartless
sun
that rides above

I think
the moon
has been much easier
to praise

and I think
that today
I must follow
my heart

while the smoke
is less
and I am not confronted
by air
that hangs so near
and almost
in my face

it is a day to walk

before the sun
is high

and I will go
to take my fill
of the township
while it still stands

just as
for me
it has always stood

I'll take my fill
of post office corner

and a moment
with the pigeons there

the ford street fountain

and the dolphin
café

small pieces
of me
from my childhood
and the
long ago

and
I may touch
I think

to feel the texture

perhaps
embrace

the elder apple-box tree

streets of elms
and the stand
of poplars

a trickling
moment
by the laughing creek

I fished there
once
for small trout

and smoked
my
small cigarettes

dreamed quiet
my dreams

they were carefree
times

it seems
(I know)
that my thoughts are maudlin

and I suppose
that
that is truth

but what —
I ask you —
what am I to do

how else might I invoke
the spirits
to mind me

if not to look and see

to hear and touch
and feel
and try to *be*
in my own
so small way

the things I love

before
the flame

Frank Prem

red sun (draw a breath) go around again

the sun today
is as red
as though
it might be dying

I saw somewhere
that
is the fate
of red stars

perhaps
it is a mirror
this time

a reflection
of the earth
while the dying
abounds

I cannot bear
to recount
what I know
and
all that I have heard

the sun is red
the wind
is still

this is a day
to draw breath
before we go
around
again

because tomorrow
we go around
again

tomorrow (a little) more

we are more
now
than we were
a year ago

more
temperature

more fire

more disaster
and
more

much more
fear

and
we are less
right now
than we were
two months ago

one month
ago

just
a week

less bush
less
air

less creatures
of the forest

less trees

less bravado
(more courage)

less heart
(more stoicism)

nothing
is the same
no
thing
will be
the same

and I wonder
more

or less

about
tomorrow

what will we be

tomorrow

a little wish
toward
another day

dust (and earth) rising

I will rise
from the breath
of my own dust

swirling
alive
when the rest
is ash

different

but
I am
the same

everything has changed
yet
I
remain

and I will make
this time
myself
all new

this time
be only
a beating heart

only
the things
that will grow

and that
is all

it is enough

higher desires
seem a wish
too much

and I will sing

the breeze
will carry me
within its voice

a song of calm
that may
one day
be joy again

I long
for the days
to be joy
again

with
all voices

every one of them
a part
of the song
together
with mine

and I will
rise up

in the dust
that is
all time

loss (of everything) and sleep

he said

> well
> I thought
> I had enough
> insurance
>
> I'd covered the place
> for more
> than the cost
> and I thought
> for sure
> that would be enough
>
> but
> it seems as though
> it is never
> quite as much
> as you first thought
>
> and
> it seems as though
> the costs
> are always
> more
>
> the bank claimed
> first
> to get money back
> for the mortgage
>
> then
> well
> they changed the re-building rules
> you know
>
> just
> to make things better

*to make sure
houses in the bush
are built
much stronger
next time around*

ha

*ha
ha*

*as though
any kind of strong
could withstand
a fire
like this one was*

anyway . . .

anyway . . .

*I ended up
in debt again
then
I found my business
was in strife*

*no customers
no visitors*

no tourists

for much too long

*I had to leave it
behind*

*and the memories I hold
of that
have become
strange places*

*it feels as though
it all happened
to someone else*

Of Drought And Fire

I don't know
the way it works
but
I've started waking up
in the night
again

and in the middle
of the darkness
the flames
and what I lost
are all this one
thing

the same thing

sometimes
I think
I may never get to sleep
again

blood moon (who cares)

I call the name
of the moon

she is red
in the sky

looking down
from above

I want
to ask her
why

I speak her name
softly

only loud enough
to let her know
I am watching
and wondering

my face
is bathed
in her glow

and I ponder . . .

does she know
who I am

does she even know
that I care
enough
to call her name

so softly

enough
to look at her
up there

listen to (the reddest and most silent)

on the smokiest
day

beneath the reddest
sun

I sing
a canary song

listen
to me
sing

I trill it
aloud
so you can hear

then
I draw another breath

take it deep
inside myself

change it
transform it
so that
your ears might hear

have you
the ears
to hear me
as my voice
grows quiet and still

holds no
power

no
no power no more

but it *sounds*
in just the way
that silence
should sound

and I ask again

I ask you
one more time

do you have the ears
to hear me when
no song of mine
remains

just a smoke filled day
hiding
beneath the reddest sun
I have ever seen

that perhaps
has ever been

perhaps
you still need
to listen

the way (of the dinosaurs)

oh god
the sun

that used to show
such
mellow hues

has coloured all
the earth

a cloud
that was
once
eucalypt

is a girdle
tight

and the sun sets
red
wherever

wherever it
may fall

I
think I know
the way
of the dinosaurs

choked
to death
on spittle
that once upon
a time
was air

who can breathe
this stuff

who can
live
in this stuff

fires
are temporary
but the *stuff*
you know . . .

stuff
is forever

ever
ever it is

for
ever

and so

we go the way
of the dinosaurs

a girdle of smoke

and cloud

and spittle that
cannot
be breathed

with (headache) air in mind

breathing headache air
at
three ay-em

it crept in
underneath
the hallway door

and squeezed around
the rubber seal
that keeps the window
closed

there is no way
to sleep
through this
when the particles are up
and dancing

I try to read
the midnight news

already
I am out
of date

I find that I can't help
but feel
the world has moved
while I
was trying
so hard
to remain asleep

who remembers flame
today

it was
already yesterday
when we were burned

who can see the past
through the grey
of air
that smoulders
while it covers up the worst
of sights

>   *the fire-black*
>   *of the bush . . .*
>
>   *of everything*

then seeps indoors
as headache air
underneath each doorway

around the seals of windows
then settles
inside my mind

deeply I carry (a full tide)

the world
is awash

from the humbling
of the forests
to the sky
above
and then
at the whim
of the breeze

the grey cloud
is swimming
in its own way
in
and out

and far away
until . . .

it returns

with the smell
of the dead
carried along
with it

taking grief
without requiem
to all the places
it goes

is that
creature

is it
tree
is it the hope
that my heart held

who knows

whatever it was
it is gone
now

doomed ever and anon
to return
as an odour
as a whiff
of charnel

I would forget it
you know
if I could

turn my back —
hardened —
against it

but
it comes
when I
least expect it

filling my mouth
my nose
and my lungs

and my night

until it fills
up
my mind

and whether I like it
or no

whether the wind
blows it
for a moment
or no

or
no

no

I carry it now
everywhere
as a part
of me

no need (to weep)

through the night
a gathering
of foul
perched above my head
where I lay
sleeping

and I felt it
as a gentle wheeze
each time
I took a breath

and I felt it
as a tear that fell
from my eyes —
each
in turn —
without my knowledge
and without
a provocation

though
my dreams were strange

troubled
by this grey moment
in time
and who is to say
that is not a reason
and enough
for a casual cry

~

I carry a picture
of myself
within my mind

Of Drought And Fire

the image
is of me
as a hollow mannequin

filling up
in shades
of damaged air

that rises within me
from the ground

not filled up
completely

not yet

only as high
as my chest

as high
as that part of me
that does the breathing

~

I am weary of feeling
like this

I am wearied
by knowing
that the awareness
of this
will not end

no

not today

perhaps there will be
no need
to weep
tomorrow

the joke

I have been taken
down
by the hoax
of a prankster

who suggested hope
when none
was there

he whispered *rain*

he suggested
downpour

but the moment
came

and went

I am still
waiting

the filtered sun
shows
the whole world
through a pall

a metaphor that is (a dying star)

in the clarity
of
a sultry night

I see the stars
by smoke
unveiled

betelgeuse
they say
is growing red
before
its dying

I can't see that
cannot see beyond
the map
that warns
of fire
down below

but I watch the stars
I watch
and wonder
which
is betelgeuse

which one of them
is red
and dying

is it somewhere near
mount buffalo

somewhere near
merrimbula
or
mogo

maybe batlow

maybe
anywhere
at all
that is terrestrial

perhaps
betelgeuse
is just
a metaphor

a week is a long time (is no time)

I guess
it always happens

I guess that
this
is *how* it happens

guess
a week has gone by
already

and the news
that's in the papers
wants to *love*
the minister
and
wants to *hate*
the minister

and social media
already knows
who *has* to go

who *must* be
punished

the stories
are growing
day by day

there is going to be
some hardship
but
the argument is all about
money yes
and money no

who and what
and where

it is as though
something
might have happened
in a bad dream

a different kind
of surreal

and then today
after the rain
didn't come

the fire map
sprang back to life

mount buffalo
down
to myrtleford

and suddenly
there is no time

pretty (was)

it is a pretty
little town

here we are
on main street

the municipal offices
rise proud
halfway down
the block

that shop
there
is the newsagent

across the road
the pharmacy
six days
a week

bakery buns
are a treat

they make pink
lamingtons

on every major corner
there is a pub
this town
has a thirst
you know

and the gardens
(memorial)
are a hundred
and fifty
years old

*bunya pines
with their prickle leaves
rise up
into the sky*

*the next street
down
has the oldest houses*

*weatherboard walls
and tin roofs
on a quarter acre*

*elm trees
are still the civic pride*

*and the streets
are long*

*paved
with bitumen*

*the kids can play
on the forest reserve
like their parents
did*

*and theirs
before them*

*kids
can play
like they always
could*

*they will play
around here
I think
forever*

~

Of Drought And Fire

this used to be
a town

you can see
this
was a street

all the patches

the ash patches
were buildings
once

and you can tell
what was the main-drag
and
what's left
of where the shops
were

twisted tin

a few bricks

wisps rising
from suspicious looking
mounds

they could be
anything

I believe
they had a long line
of old trees
here

you can see
it's a sort of
rectangle
of about an acre

nothing there now
so
I might be wrong

all the way
along this road
the tar
has melted

schools
are gone

all
the old houses

this is
a war zone

with nothing left
but
discoloured rectangles
of
around about
a quarter acre

the forest —
those few sticks there —
is still
smouldering

I suppose
they must have
let it grow
too close

no problem now
though

it is gone
for good

a dusting of brown (turning into black)

I thought the smoke
that rose
from the fire
was enough

of and by itself
it took over
all our lives

breathing the death
of our forests
was . . .

confronting

and I felt as low
as a person
who holds
such things
in his heart
can feel

but
in a world of
one-off
astonishments
and dismay laid-on

I should not
be surprised
there is always
one more thing

the topsoil
of new south wales
has risen up
to the sky

a cloud of dust
starts grey
then turns
to brown

turns itself
into billows

and day
into the black
of night

my town (still pretty)

somehow
I have stayed pretty
so far

just
so far

the ravage around me
has not landed
has not touched

pretty much
I am
as
pretty much
I was

beauty
is just
a point of view

I know it depends
on what you look for

and somehow
I seem
still
to be pretty
while those around
wear blackened shades
of dust and sour ash

maybe
it is because
I am built of stone

on granite
deep
into the bones

*I don't know
but
I am pretty
still
even when I
am weeping

for the ones
all
the other ones
that are gone

could
every one of them
have been
me*

a song of rain (a hint of thunder)

cover me
with kisses
baby

roar sweet things
into my ear

tenderly

take me
in your arms

let us spin
on the dampness
of the concrete path

beside the back door

I want to see you
falling
drop by drop

I want you
so much
that I . . .

I . . .

can't stop myself
from dancing

splashing
with my feet
and dancing

rising (but) beyond song

rising up
out of the dirt
out of the ashes
I am hurting

some places
I bleed

but
how can I know
I am alive
without feeling that

it is the blood
that flows to make me
what I am

so I rise

and so
I stand

unsteady
I know you know
that I could use
some small assistance

but I stagger on

will always
stagger on

not what I
once
used to be

not what I
once believed

I had better get used
to not being
the image
that I hold in my head

that me
is a memory

a mirage shimmer
on the edge
of sight

a vision
of *was*
that visits
sometimes
in the deep
darkness

bang the sticks
for me
bang
and bang
the rhythm sticks

chant the songs

it is only
singing
that will keep
my any where
any part
my any thing
strong

so sing for me

sing
sing
sing for me now

of life

and
of being

the healing
of my bones

only
my bones

the flesh of me
is gone
beyond

howl (and cry)

a shrouded moon

only
a sliver
of itself

low down
in the western sky

the veil she wears
to me
seems mourning

for how

how can it be
that
when someone . . .

some *thing*

so close to you
has died
a new day
still rises
with the sun
and forgets the moon
and her sliver cloak
of shrouding

forgets
the night
entire

something else
comes

something else
needs

something
takes their place

a stranger
seated at the table
there

right there

a different shape
in the familiar setting
as though
it has always been
and
nothing has changed

when everything
has changed

let us go
you and I
to a place where we can look up
to see the sky

there
let us howl

and there
let us cry

howl and cry
until
we are emptied

the news (that haunts)

I hear the screams
sometimes
in my imagination

mostly
maybe
when the lights go out

after a day
absorbing
what they call
the news

I hear the screams
in the darkness
sometimes

released
to haunt the flames
of blackened dreams

the edge is a bruise (from space)

looking down
from space
where the satellites
reside

it seems
just a bruise

grey
in the sky

black
on the ground

red . . .

still red
around too many
edges

but
it is not
like a bruise
when it grows
and
it grows

not like a bruise
in the way
it keeps spreading
or
when a hot day
brings
a hotter wind

and
you are standing too close
because
it comes

Of Drought And Fire

for *you*

too fast . . .

~

I suppose
that might be
the problem
with a view
that is too wide
and taken
from too far away

from
out in space
where it is so hard to see
small people

like you

and me

caught
by the red
that is still burning
all
of the edges

lies spoken softly (in centigrade)

twenty-nine
centigrade

who would
believe it

eighty-four in fahrenheit

that is as low
as it goes

as low
as it went

it was a hot night
in my town
last night

I should not
complain

at least
we could breathe
the air

I kept
imagining —
in the half-doze
that was the best
I could
do —
kept imagining
little patter-drops
of rain

but I think
it was the sound
of the tin roof
over the veranda

Of Drought And Fire

contracting
and expanding
like lungs
trying to work out
a sigh

interrupted
from time
to time

by a noise
that sounded
halfway
between a low groan
and a cry

that
was the sound of me
not quite
close enough
to sleeping

and when I walked outside
I stepped into
a slow oven

the pizza-cooked
residual air
left behind

and I walked onto
a patch of grass
that felt alien
in the dark

as though the dry
of the heat
had taken the plant
away

and left plastic
in its place

coarse plastic
never seen
never softened
by rain . . .

it is going to be
hell
today

I can see it
in the morning
light

the breeze
is a lie

the cloud
is a lie

the only truth
I think
is melting
beneath
the sun

I can hardly
stay awake
but
even the promise
of sleep
is nothing but
a lie

canberra

there is an emergency
in canberra

usually
it would be
about politics
at its worst

and there *is*
a bit of that around

but today they are
quietly pronouncing
warnings

conjuring up memories
of the year two thousand
and three
when they burned

oh lord
didn't they burn
back then

> *I make this*
> *declaration . . .*
>
> *especially*
> *for south tuggeranong . . .*
>
> *I understand*
> *your state of high*
> *anxiety . . .*
>
> *but*
> *the ororral valley fire*
> *has already burned*
>
> *eight percent*
> *of all the land*
> *that we have*

*go
or stay
it is time for you
to decide*

on the map
there is a flower
shaded pink
and red

you'd think it
a part
of some bouquet

but canberra
is in a state
of dire warning

left dry (and unworldly)

how will we drink
the dust

can you tell me

we are burning
from above
draining
from below

there'll be nothing left
soon
but the holes
where we mined the water
and the cracks
in the earth
that were once held together
by it

and *still* it is not
enough

we have to take
another barrel out

send it
all the way
to china

like taking
your own heart
and selling it
to the highest bidder

leaving *you*
behind
like a husk
after harvest

rattling empty
with every breeze
that passes
where we are left
to stand

a ragged bunch
of scarecrow skeletons
still craving

not knowing
yet
that we have already
died

and that the dead
can no more serve
any
worldly purpose

a small one weeping (near diffey road)

it was only
a small one

a black flame
on the map

a symbol beside it
to indicate

> *responding*

just a small one
on diffey road
but
enough
to colour the moon

we stood
and stared
as the bleeding thing
crept out
from behind
a cloud

a reflection
from above
of our
below

and as the wind
swept by
shrill
and filled with howling
I thought I heard
from somewhere
not far
from diffey road
the sound
of weeping

permafrost rising (at three o'clock)

do you wake
in the night
wondering
if the climate
is still
in place

or
if you might rise
in the morning
to fire

maybe to
just the smoke
of something you knew
now burned

or the taste
of ash
blown here
from a hundred miles
away

so very far
away . . .

so close

like the climate
in the night
shining out
so brightly
on social media
where you may learn
that

the permafrost
is gone

all the gases
in siberia
are rising

right up
into the sky

and
everyone is lying

I believe

yes
everyone
is lying

but
at three o'clock
I am awake
and wondering
about
no good
tomorrow

la la (just listen)

I will not say
that I danced
naked

but
when the sound
of fattened raindrops
falling
filtered through my mind
to wake me
at first I lay
as still as though
I was in
a coma

then
I quickly rose
and walked
in darkness
through the house

to the back door
and
the outside

I stood
for awhile

drew breath
filtered clean
by the falling rain

la la lala

listen

just listen

the sound
of falling rain

a koala (in the coalmine)

mike
wrote a letter

said

> I have paid the staff
> I have paid the rent
> I have paid the superannuation
> I have paid the workers compensation
> I have paid the property rates
>
> but
> I am not sure
> now
> how I can pay
> for stock
> to put into the store
>
> and
> in any case
> most of the tourists
> left the town
> on january the third
>
> told me they thought
> it might be better
> to be safe
> than to end up
> crying
> or dying
>
> and I wonder
> on a wednesday
> in middle february
>
> will they come back
> this year

I talked to ross
across the bar
at the local pub

he told me

>it is . . .

>. . . only temporary
>but
>the dining room
>is closed

>you can eat out here
>in the main bar

>it is
>the very same food

>very same
>quality

>but
>I can't open up
>for a room filled
>with empty tables
>and silent chairs

>on too many days
>now
>we have only
>silent chairs

the news on tv
is still filled up
with koala bears
and wombats

and scandal
and sport

three wombats
sharing one bowl

a mention

Of Drought And Fire

of the birds
that remain

maybe reference
to the ones
that are gone

and great woe
at the thought
of an extinction

wails
and woes
at the thought
of a koala bear
extinction

and the question
that arises
is not
if it will
but
when it will

so
will it be the koala
lost
from the cage
in our coalmine

will it be
a fish-kill
in the river
instead

or maybe
mike
in his shop
of sundry
mixed goods

perhaps ross
behind the bar

there are days
now
when I no longer hear
the koala sing

drowning (in lessons)

there is a cyclone
approaching queensland

rolling
from up there
down
toward new south wales

burning
from september

and drowning
in february

can he catch
a breath . . .

can *anyman*

anywoman

please please
catch a breath

.
.
.

please

there are lessons
being taught
I know

lessons being learned
maybe
(that is less certain)

but
how can I . . .

anybody

take it in
when
there is a cyclone
now
following on
from last week's deluge

and a chance
that even
the best of lessons
might be drowned

From the News: https://www.gympietimes.com.au/news/monster-storm-on-collision-course/3942411/

After Words

Index of Poems

A

a bucket standard 83
a departure by the boy child 53
a dusting of brown (turning into black) 213
a funny game 17
ageing optimism 67
a koala (in the coalmine) 237
all taken (by the day) 176
a metaphor that is (a dying star) 205
and we become (the thing that we denied) a refugee 111
a (prime) ministerial (possible) message 130
a small one weeping (near diffey road) 233
a smoke shroud (of change) 167
a song of rain (a hint of thunder) 217
a strange season 71
a streaky river (for my face) 109
a week is a long time (is no time) 207

B

back-burn lottery 50
bitter 147
blood moon (who cares) 192
blue and black and the bridge (on fire) 118

C

canberra 229
carol birds 60
claustrophobic smog (cry the cockatoo) 169

D

deeply I carry (a full tide) 199
deserving (better) 125
different rivers 29
dirty dreams and dry 10
doing fruit 20
dreaming 122

drowning (in lessons) 241
dust (and earth) rising 187

F

factual oblivion 26

H

heartbeat (leadership) 148
hope rage 63
hope risen (from a single fall of rain) 47
howl (and cry) 221
hungry 159

L

lagoon #01 9
lagoon #02 11
lagoon #03 16
lagoon #04 19
lagoon #05 22
lagoon #06 25
lagoon #07 28
lagoon #08 31
lagoon #09 33
lagoon #10 37
lagoon #11 41
lagoon #12 - zen fish 44
lagoon #13 46
lagoon #14 49
lagoon #15 52
lagoon #16 54
lagoon #17 58
lagoon #18 62
lagoon #19 65
lagoon #20 68
lagoon #21 70
lagoon #22 72
lagoon #23 75
lagoon #24 79
lagoon #25 82
lagoon #26 84
lagoon #27 88

lagoon #28 92
lagoon #29 96
lagoon #30 100
lagoon #31 103
la la (just listen) 236
left dry (and unworldly) 231
lies spoken softly (in centigrade) 226
listen to (the reddest and most silent) 193
looking away (from a trip I took) 133
loss (of everything) and sleep 189

M

mellish street (tomorrow) 114
more like custard 40
my town (still pretty) 215

N

no drought 76
no need (to weep) 202
no one (she said) 161
normal (now) 171
normal wonder 94
not here (when we burn) 142

P

parched harvest 98
permafrost rising (at three o'clock) 234
please 146
pray for (a bottle of) rain 136
pretty (was) 209

R

rain child 73
rain traces 86
red sun (draw a breath) go around again 184
rising (but) beyond song 218
rocket seeds and a helpful drip 56

S

salvation (before the distribution of voting preferences) 80
sated 163
seamless liquidity 32
seasonal content 101
something (really) 128

T

the 101 ways (#79) 164
the battle (do or . . .) 153
the blessing of (two mls) of rain 178
the edge is a bruise (from space) 224
the farmer's march 90
the fog price 169
the good news 23
the joke 204
the news (that haunts) 223
the way (of the dinosaurs) 195
to be (before the flame) 180
tomorrow (a little) more 185
two heats 69

W

watching weather (in time for christmas) 45
we will bicker (until tomorrow comes) 139
what I heard today 35
what may come (we shall see) 156
with (headache) air in mind 197
worry yes (but just a little pleasure) 173
wrongness and sun 43

Y

yellow mellow: desiccation north 13

Author Information

Frank Prem has been a storytelling poet since his teenage years. He has been a psychiatric nurse through all of his professional career, which now exceeds forty years.

He has been published in magazines, online zines, and anthologies in Australia, and in a number of other countries, and has both performed and recorded his work as spoken word.

Frank is an Adjunct Research Associate of the School of Education, Charles Sturt University, Australia.

He lives with his wife in the beautiful township of Beechworth in North East Victoria, Australia.

Connect with Frank

Find Frank at his website www.FrankPrem.com, or through Social Media online at Facebook, X (Twitter), Instagram and YouTube.

Other Published Works

Free Verse Poetry

Small Town Kid (2018)
Devil In The Wind (2019)
The New Asylum (2019)
Herja, Devastation - With Cage Dunn (2019)
Walk Away Silver Heart (2020)
A Kiss for the Worthy (2020)
Rescue and Redemption (2020)
Pebbles to Poems (2020)
The Garden Black (2022)
A Specialist at The Recycled Heart (2022)
Ida: Searching for The Jazz Baby (2023)
From Volyn to Kherson (2023)
Alive Is What You Feel (2023)
White Whale (2024)
Pilgrim Volume 1 - Illustrated by Leanne Murphy (2024)
A Poetry Archive Volume 1 (2024)
A Poetry Archive Volume 2 (2024)
A Poetry Archive Volume 3 (2024)
A Poetry Archive Volume 4 (2024)

Picture Poetry/Spoken Image

Voices (In The Trash) (2020)
The Beechworth Bakery Bears (2021)
Sheep On The Somme (2021)
Waiting For Frank-Bear (2021)
A Lake Sambell Walk (2021)
A Few Places Near Home (2023)
The Cielonaut (2024)

What Readers Say

Small Town Kid

A modern-day minstrel. Highly recommended.
—A. F. (Australia)

Small Town Kid is a wonderful collection.
—S. T. (Australia)

Devil In The Wind

Trust me, this book will stay with you. Bravo!
—K. K. (USA)

Moving, beautiful, and terrible. I was left with a profound sense of respect, as well as a reminder that we should never take for granted every precious every moment of life.
—J. S. (South Africa)

The New Asylum

Words can't do justice to the emotional journey I travelled in (reading this collection).
—C. D. (Australia)

If I had to pick one book over the past year that has truly resonated with me, this would be it.
—K. B. (USA)

Walk Away Silver Heart

Instantly grips you by the throat in his step-by-step story of survival. Bravo!
—K. K. (USA)

Outstanding!
—B. T. (Australia)

A Kiss For The Worthy

A Celebration of Life Written in Thoughtful Bursts of Poetic Expression
—C M C (United States)

With every verse, I found myself reflecting about myself, my life, and the world.
—K

Rescue and Redemption

The passion of love in its many forms explored by one for another.
—J L (United States)

I've enjoyed every word, every breath. Every moment within the life of these stories.
—C D (Australia)

Sheep On The Somme

Museums and archivists take note~sell this in your gift shops, preserve it in your archives. Professors, teachers~share with your students.
—A R C (United States)

(This) book is a beautiful and graphic tribute to all those brave men and women who gave their lives for their countries between 1914 and 1918.
—R C (South Africa)

Ida: Searching for The Jazz Baby

I found myself deeply moved by the presentation of Ida's elusive, illusionary life.
—E G (United States)

He gives her a depth and vulnerability that the press didn't.
— A C (United Kingdom

The Garden Black

Prem creates verse that illuminates our world, its experiences and history.
—S C (United Kingdom)

Prem's poetry reminds that life is fragile and fleeting ... both harsh and beautiful.
—D G K (Canada)

A Few Places Near Home

The author has captured many beautiful images in this book, and is a wonderful photographer as well as a poet. This book would make a beautiful coffee table book filled with moving prose to make us ponder with gorgeous accompanying images.
—D K (Canada)

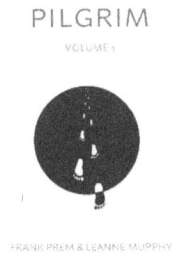

www.FrankPrem.com

www.ingramcontent.com/pod-product-compliance
Lightning Source LLC
Chambersburg PA
CBHW050157130526
44590CB00044B/3376